Cat

This book belongs to:

I0410794

Paws & Claws

Animals &
Their Tracks
Coloring Book

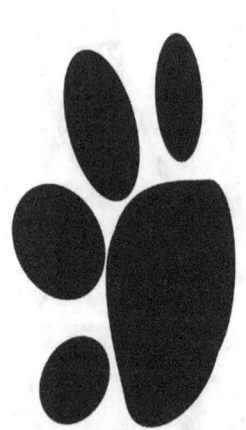

Mary Lou Brown
Sandy Mahony

Human Girl

Copyright ©2017 Mary Lou Brown & Sandy Mahony

All rights reserved. No part of this book may be reproduced in any form or by any electronic or mechanical means including information storage and retrieval systems, without permission in writing from the authors. The only exception is by a reviewer, who may quote short excerpts in a review.

Monkey

Monkey

Turtle

Turtle

Elephant

Elephant

Cow

Cow

Zebra

Horse

Bear

Bear

Dog

Dog

Pig

Pig

Frog

Frog

Crocodile

Crocodile

Duck

Duck

Tiger

Tiger

Chicken
Rooster

Chicken
Hen

Giraffe

Giraffe

Gecko

Gecko

Deer

Deer

Human
Boy

adventurelearningpress.com

www.ingramcontent.com/pod-product-compliance
Lightning Source LLC
Chambersburg PA
CBHW081804280526
45789CB00008B/2990